LITTLE IS MUCH IN

THE MASTER'S

HANDS

Maximizing Your God-given Potential

by

Ursula T. Burroughs

Copyright Notice

Ursula T. Burroughs
Little is Much in the Master's Hands
Maximizing Your God-given Potential

© 2016, Ursula T. Burroughs
Anointed Fire™ House
Email: uburroughs@yahoo.com

DEDICATION

This book is dedicated to every person who feels the stirring of greatness on the inside of them, but have yet to tap into it. I encourage you to push until you birth your purpose.

ACKNOWLEDGMENTS

I would like to thank my Heavenly Father for using me as a vessel to share His truths with the world. Without His divine inspiration, this book would not have been birthed.

I am thankful to my wonderful parents, James and Evelyn George, who have encouraged and cheered me on during the entire process of writing this book: I love you guys and I am forever grateful to have you both in my corner.

To the woman of God, Tiffany Buckner, who has been my mentor and mid-wife during this journey: Thank you for allowing God to use you. You are truly a blessing to the body of Christ.

Sincere thanks to my Pastor, Patrick E. Winfield, of The Potter's House Fort Worth:

Thank you for pouring into me and helping me to walk in my purpose through your in-depth teaching of the Word of God and your amazing leadership.

TABLE OF CONTENTS

Introduction...IX

Chapter 1...

The Seed of Potential 1

Chapter 2...

I Wasn't Born Just to Pay Bills and Die...5

Chapter 3...

Changing Your Mind and Your Mouth......9

Chapter 4...

Complete Surrender.............................15

Chapter 5...

The Heart of the Matter........................23

Chapter 6...

A Hard Head Can Hinder 31

Chapter 7...

Four Potential Killers............................37

Chapter 8...

Pregnant with Purpose.........................47

Chapter 9...

Labor Pains...59

Chapter 10...

P.U.S.H...65

Chapter 11...

Six Hindrances to Prayer......................77

Chapter 12..

How to Fuel Your Potential....................87

Chapter 13..

Connected for Purpose.........................97

Chapter 14..

Don't Give Up......................................107

Chapter 15..

Your Purpose Matters for Eternity........119

INTRODUCTION

Trying to discover my purpose in life had been something that I struggled with for many years. After going off to college, earning a few of degrees, and finally settling into a stable career as a Physical Therapist, I began to feel a sense of discomfort and lack of fulfillment in what I was doing. By all means, I was and still am grateful for the opportunity to help others in that particular line of work, but I knew that there was something greater on the inside me. I knew that my life had more to it than the day-to-day ritual of working and coming home. I knew that what I was doing was something that I had chosen for myself and not exactly what God had chosen for me. I couldn't envision the current state of my life as it was to be the end-all, be-all. For several years, I became frustrated as I waited for God to reveal what He ultimately called me to do. I would often become restless in my mind and unable to relax my thoughts as it pertained to me fulfilling the unknown purpose on the inside of me.

One day, while taking a short nap, I began to pray and ask God why I felt so discontent in my spirit and the Holy Spirit gently responded to me. He told me that I was experiencing labor pains and that I would be giving birth to my purpose soon.

Potential is on the inside of every human being and it has been given to us by God to help us live out our purpose in the earth. It's not about how much potential you start with, but it's what you make of it. The disciples didn't have much potential to feed the multitude of five thousand people. All they had were two fish and five loaves of bread, but when they handed what they had over to Jesus, He blessed it and it became more than enough and fed many people *(see Matthew14:15-21)*.

Little is much when placed in the hands of the Almighty. If you give your potential over to God, there is no limit to what He is able to do in and through you. Surrender your life completely to God and walk in your purpose. You will never experience true contentment when you are not fully living your purpose and maximizing all of the amazing potential that God has placed on the inside of you.

Chapter 1
THE SEED OF POTENTIAL

Everything that God has created has been given a seed or measure of potential. How and if that seed ever develops is up to the one to whom it has been given. Merriam-Webster's dictionary defines potential as: *an ability that someone has that can be developed to help that person become successful.* I like to define potential as untapped possibility. The possibility for greatness lies within the belly of each and every human being, but in order to fully tap into that greatness, we must first have an understanding and relationship with the One who has given us this amazing gift.

In order for a seed to grow, it must be fertilized. As seeds begin to receive proper nutrients such as sunlight and water, they begin to grow into something bigger and greater. Your potential is your seed and the nutrient needed to grow it is the Word of God. Without proper nutrients from the life-giving Word of God, your potential will never manifest to its fullest expression in the earth.

The book of Matthew 13:14-29 talks about the parable of the Three Servants. The scripture provides a clear understanding of how God views the potential He has given each of us and what He expects us to do with it. In the parable, each servant was given a particular amount of money based on his ability and was instructed to be a good steward over it until the Master returned from his trip. The servant who was given five bags of silver invested it and earned five more; the servant with two bags of silver invested his and earned two more, but the servant with one bag of silver dug a hole and hid his. When the Master returned from his trip, each servant had to give an account of how they used the money he had given them. The servants who had been given two bags and five bags of silver had both doubled their investments. The Master was very well pleased and praised them both for being wise stewards over what he had given them. He assured them that because of their faithfulness in handling such a small amount that he would allow them to be stewards over much more. The servant who was given one bag of silver was too afraid to invest what he had been given. The Master referred to him as being lazy and wicked and ended up giving his one bag of silver to the servant who now had ten. *"To those who use well what they are given, even more will be given, and they will have an abundance. But from those who do nothing, even what little they have will be taken away"* *(Matthew 13:29 NLT).* God expects us to be wise stewards over the potential He has given us. We were not created to just sit around and live in mediocrity. Jesus came that we might have an abundant life (see John 10:10), meaning that we lack nothing; that we live in an overflow of our highest and fullest God-given potential.

Chapter 2
I WASN'T BORN JUST TO PAY BILLS AND DIE

Many people can attest to the frustration of the repetitive day-in and day-out cycle of going to work, coming home, and paying bills. After years and years of doing this, it can begin to seem as though this repetitive insanity is all there is to life. I personally began to feel this way about five years into my career as a Physical Therapist. I had accumulated a large student loan debt from attending undergraduate school and going back to graduate school for two Masters degrees. The reality of it seemed as though I had gone to school only to learn how to master being a slave to debt. I knew deep down on the inside of me that there was more to my life than that.

There was no way God spent all that time creating me with such intricate detail and great purpose, for me to be living to pay back Sallie Mae and all her counterparts. I knew that God had an awesome plan and purpose for my life and I just had to tap into it.

"For I know the plans I have for you," says the Lord. "They are plans for good and not for disaster, to give you a future and a hope. "In those days when you pray, I will listen. If you look for me wholeheartedly, you will find me. I will be found by you," says the Lord. "I will end your captivity and restore your fortunes. I will gather you out of the nations where I sent you and will bring you home again to your own land" (Jeremiah 29:11-14 NLT).

God has an expected end for all of His children. When He looks at us, He sees all of the potential and possibilities He has placed on the inside of us. It is not His desire that we live beneath our potential and the calling He has placed on our lives. He beckons us to seek Him with all of our hearts and He tells us that in doing so, we will find Him. We are held in confinement by the mundane routine of working and paying bills with death presenting itself as a false exit strategy to our misery. God has promised that He would end our captivity and restore our fortunes if we pray and are committed to seeking Him out.

It has been said that the grave is the most creative place on earth and is filled with the most potential. I believe this to be true because there are so many people like the servant with the one bag of silver, who keep their potential hidden and never maximize it. Just think, the cure for AIDS and cancer could be buried six feet deep, all because someone was too afraid to step out and trust the potential God had placed on the inside of them.

I am a big follower of Evangelist Joyce Meyer's teaching and I remember hearing her say that "Just because you feel fear doesn't mean you can't do it. Do it afraid." This statement is true for those of you who are living stagnated lives and are too afraid to step out into your God-given purpose. Just give whatever it is that God is calling for you to do a try. The worst thing that could happen is that you actually succeed!

Chapter 3
CHANGING YOUR MIND AND YOUR MOUTH

"Don't copy the behavior and customs of this world, but let God transform you into a new person by changing the way you think. Then you will learn to know God's will for you, which is good and pleasing and perfect" (Romans 12:2 NLT).

Your life does not have the power to change if your mind stays the same. If you continue to go around thinking that you were born to pay bills and die, that is exactly what you will do. Your thoughts and your words have to line up with the Word of God to experience the full manifestation of your purpose in the earth. You

have to trust and follow the blueprint of the
One who created you.

There are many older adults who haven't
tapped into their potential and feel as though
it's too late to start. Recently, I spoke with a 60-
year-old woman who works in the healthcare
industry and I asked her if she felt that she was
living up to her fullest potential. Her response
was "No." She went on to say that she felt as
though she had become too old to try and do
anything different than what she had been
doing. I assured her that it is never too late for
her to maximize her potential. As long as there
is breath in your body, the opportunity is still
there, but it takes a changed mindset in order
to move forward. Stop allowing your potential
to be buried underneath your insecurities.
Common insecurities include age, education
level, socioeconomic status, appearance, and
so on. The more you draw closer to God, the

more you will be able to see yourself as He sees you.

"The tongue can bring death or life; those who love to talk: will reap the consequences" (Proverbs 18:21 NLT).

Get out of the habit of saying what you "can't do" and start saying what you "can do." The words you speak over yourself are so powerful that they can bring death or life to you. Many people don't realize that the state in which they find themselves in is primarily due to the words they have spoken over themselves, whether they be good or bad. From this day forward, start professing the following statement over yourself daily: "God put great potential on the inside of me. By grace and through faith, I will live in the fullness of it." If you know specifically what it is that God has placed in you or is calling you to do, you should begin to profess that out loud each day as well. Your outward profession is an act of faith. Although you have not seen what you are speaking come into full manifestation, you are expressing that you believe it will come to pass.

"So you see, faith by itself isn't enough. Unless it produces good deeds, it is dead and useless" (James 2:17 NLT).

Now that your mouth has had its makeover, you must put actions with everything you have spoken. It is not enough to offer lip service and say that you have the potential for success, but don't pray and seek God's face or read His Word for guidance. You must also put forth some type of effort in the area in which you believe God is calling you to. For example, if you believe the potential that you have been sitting on is the gift of writing, you could start writing your own blog. Just this small effort on your part could turn into you writing and publishing your first book. All it takes is a little bit of faith to make things turn around. *"If you had faith even as small as a mustard seed, you could say to this mulberry tree, 'May you be uprooted and thrown into the sea,' and it would obey you" (Luke 17:6 NLT).*

Your mind is a battlefield where Satan wages war against your purpose and your soul. There is no possible way you can win without having God on your side. There is no possible way you can walk in your purpose without being connected to the author and perfecter of your faith. *"...And let us run with endurance the race God has set before us. We do this by keeping our eyes on Jesus, the champion who initiates and perfects our faith" (12:1-2 NLT)*

Chapter 4
COMPLETE SURRENDER

Many people are familiar with the way in which GPS (Global Positioning System) works. You type in your desired destination and it provides you with turn-by-turn directions on how to get there. If you get turned around or miss your exit, it will re-route you back on course in order to get you where you need to be. If your route is congested with traffic or an accident, the GPS will give you an alternate direction. What I like most about GPS is its ability to provide me with an ETA (estimated time of arrival). This feature allows me to manage my time in terms of whether or not I have a few minutes to stop for gas or grab a coffee before making it to my destination at the scheduled time. Although the GPS provides you with direction, it still allows the driver to control the destination. As a matter of fact, the driver is in complete control because he or she can decrease the speed, make stops, change the destination, or even shut the GPS system off altogether. Think of God as your personal GPS (God's Perfect System), but with you losing complete control over the destination and the ETA. The GPS of God determined your destiny long before you were ever formed in your mother's womb. *"I knew you before I formed you in your mother's womb. Before you were born, I set you apart and appointed you as my prophet to the nations" (Jeremiah 1:5 NLT).* God doesn't need your help when it comes to destiny. All He needs you to do is surrender your will to Him.

A life surrendered to Christ calls for you to let go of every preconceived idea of what you think your life should be, how you think it should go, and when you think it should go that way. The what, how, and when of your life is not determined by you, so let it go. Holding on to your will keeps God from being able to manifest His perfect will in your life.

The children of Israel taking forty years to make what was supposed to be a forty-day journey to the promised land is a great example of what a life not fully submitted and surrendered to God looks like. When we refuse to listen to the voice of God and try to re-route His direction in our lives, we are left to go our own way and end up never maximizing our God-given potential.

"But as surely as I live, and as surely as the earth is filled with the Lord's glory, not one of these people will ever enter that land. They have all seen my glorious presence and the miraculous signs I performed both in Egypt and in the wilderness, but again and again, they

have tested me by refusing to listen to my voice. They will never even see the land I swore to give their ancestors. None of those who have treated me with contempt will ever see it. But my servant Caleb has a different attitude than the others have. He has remained loyal to me so I will bring him into the land he explored" (Numbers 14:21-24 NLT).

The time that God has allotted us here on earth is swift and precious. We should allow Him to have complete control so that we can reach our destiny at his ETA. Now let me clarify that God's ETA is an "exact time of arrival." He doesn't operate within estimations of chronological time. God's timing is perfect, as He is not bound by the confines of space and time. This explains why God is able to show up with the answer to our prayers and turn things around in our lives at any given moment, unbeknownst to us.

I'm sure many people have heard the
statement, "He may not come when you want
Him, but He'll be right on time." This is
definitely true about God. I can recall many
times in my life where I have prayed for God to
do things for me at a certain time and it didn't
happen. In some cases, I ended up getting my
prayer answered years later, but I was able to
look back and see that God knew best. I would
not have been ready for the answer to that
particular prayer if it had materialized when I
wanted it to.

A person whose life is not surrendered to
Christ goes after things that God has never
intended for them to have. Doing it "my way"
like Sinatra is not in your best interest. It's
going to lead to a lot of heartache, heartbreak,
and untapped potential. Your way could cause
you to spend thirty years working as a
housekeeper, when you were called to be a

doctor, or working as a doctor when you were called to be a teacher of the Word. Don't misinterpret what I'm saying... there is nothing wrong with any of these professions, but there is something wrong with you operating in them when you were never called to. The adage: *a hard head makes a soft behind* is true when it pertains to living a life that is not fully submitted to God. You will take a beating by life when you are being disobedient to the call of God on your life and not maximizing the potential He has placed on the inside of you.

How disappointed would you be if you were to come to the end of your life and realize that you spent forty-five years stressing and struggling in the wrong career? Truth be told, I would be disappointed to realize that I have spent one year doing the wrong thing. Time is something that you will never be able to get back, so be sure to pray and seek God to determine what He would have you to do.

Psalms127:1-2 says "Unless the Lord builds a house, the work of the builders is wasted. Unless the Lord protects a city, guarding it with sentries will do no good." You have to let go and let God take control of your life. Stop wasting your time trying to create the life that you think you should have. Failure is your destiny if you take this approach to life.

Imagine seeing a headless body walking around trying to get from one place to another. You would find it bumping into stuff, going around in circles, and making absolutely no purposeful movements because it lacks its directive source…its head. In the physical sense, the head houses the eyes for vision, the brain to send instruction to the limbs on how to

accurately move, and the ears for hearing
instruction on which way to go.

When you go about life without God as your
head, you will lack vision, purpose, and the
ability to hear instruction from Him on what
steps to take. You will wonder aimlessly,
accomplishing nothing, and going absolutely
nowhere.

Decide today not to waste another moment
apart from God. Release control over yourself
into the hands of the Almighty and watch your
seed of potential blossom into a beautiful and
fruitful life of purpose.

Chapter 5
THE HEART OF THE MATTER

There is a process that has to take place when a seed grows. We usually just see the finished product that a seed produces, but there is a lot of nasty dirt, bugs, cutting away of weeds and pruning of thorns that has to be done in order for the seed to come into full manifestation of what it is supposed to be. Your seed of potential cannot thrive if your heart is unclean. If you are struggling with unforgiveness, jealousy, envy, hatred, strife, pride and lust in your heart, you must submit yourself to God and ask Him to help your overcome these things. Not only are these things killing your potential, but they are leading you to the path of eternal destruction.

In the previous chapter, we discussed the function of the head as it relates to God being in control of our lives. The heart is another vital part of bodily function. It is responsible for pumping life-sustaining blood throughout our bodies. Without it operating properly, we cannot live life at our highest level of function. Being a healthcare provider, I have come across my fair share of patients with heart disease. Many of them have heart failure, which limits the heart's ability to pump blood to other vital organs. Some of their hearts function so poorly that they lack the physical endurance and strength needed just to walk around the grocery store or up a flight of stairs. The physical state of these individuals is a reflection of the function of their hearts.

In the spiritual sense, the heart is the emotional part of our being that is fully reflected by everything that happens in our lives. *"Guard your heart above all else, for it determines the course of your life" (Proverbs 4:23 NLT).* This means that if your life is currently a mess, it's because your heart is a mess. The words you speak, whether good or bad, come from the overflow of your heart. *"A good person produces good things from the treasury of a good heart, and an evil person produces evil things from the treasury of an evil heart. What you say flows from what is in your heart" (Luke 6:45 NLT).* You will never live up to your fullest potential and purpose with a bad heart, just like you will never run the Boston Marathon with a bad heart.

Sin produces a plaque around our heart, which causes it to become hardened. A hardened heart is unable to receive anything from God because it is unrepentant and evil. An individual with a hardened heart dies a spiritual death and their natural lives are unfruitful because there is no life-sustaining blood from Jesus covering him or her.

Do a heart check. Ask God to reveal to you if there is anything in your heart that does not look like Him. Whatever He shows you, ask Him to remove it from you and cleanse your heart of all unrighteousness, so that you may live a life worthy of His call. *"And I will give you a new heart, and I will put a new spirit in you. I will take out your stony, stubborn heart and give you a tender, responsive heart. And I will put my Spirit in you so that you will follow my decrees and be careful to obey my regulations"* *(Ezekiel 36:26-27 NLT).*

We all need a heart transplant from God. As you grow in your God-given potential, be sure to ask Him to help you remain humble in heart. I say this because our flesh has a tendency to want to rise up and become prideful as God begins to elevate us. Avoid having a prideful heart at all costs. You must always realize that whatever God allows you to achieve, it is all by His grace and that He deserves all the glory for it... not you. Trust me when I say that pride will always cause you to stumble and fall. There have been many gifted people who have allowed a haughty and prideful spirit to take over.

King Nebuchadnezzar was a Babylonian King that God used to bring judgment on Judah for its disobedience, idolatry, and unfaithfulness (see Jeremiah 25:9).

God allowed Nebuchadnezzar to rise to great power and made him ruler over all the inhabited world (see Daniel 2:38), but the more he began to increase in power, the more prideful and self-absorbed he became. He made a gold statue of himself and required that all of the people of the land bow down and worship it. Those who refused to worship his statue were to be thrown into a fiery furnace (see Daniel 3:5-6). God warned Nebuchadnezzar in a dream to voluntarily humble himself or else he would undergo forced humility, be cast away from society and live among the animals. He would eat grass like a cow for seven periods of time until he learned that God is in control and that all power under heaven and earth belongs to Him (see Daniel 4:25). Apparently, Nebuchadnezzar didn't believe that God would follow through on what He said because a year after being warned, he looked out over the city of Babylon and said, *"Is not this the great Babylon I have built as the royal residence, by my mighty power and for the glory of my majesty?"* *(Daniel 4:30 NLT)* Immediately, what God said came to pass. Warning always comes before destruction. Take heed and let Nebuchadnezzar's experience with pride keep you from making the same mistake. I definitely cannot end this chapter without making note of the awesome mercy of God. Even after Nebuchadnezzar tried to exalt himself above the Almighty, once he came to his senses, God, with His infinite mercy, restored him to his position with greater than he had before (see Daniel 4:36-37).

Chapter 6
A HARD HEAD CAN HINDER

Growing up, my parents had a high level of expectation from my siblings and I when it came to doing what they instructed us to do. We were never rewarded for our disobedience. I remember times when my mother would tell us to clean our bedroom floor, and instead of doing it the way we knew she wanted it to be done, we would just sweep the middle of the floor and push all of our shoes and other junk under the bed. We would then go to bed like we had been obedient. Shortly after my mother would come in and inspect our work, she would wake us right back up to do it the correct way. Our disobedience had caused us to end up working harder than we would have if we had just followed the rules the first time.

The same holds true in each of our lives when it comes to our relationship with God. He has an expected end for our lives and instructions that He requires us to follow in order to reach that expectation. Disobedience to God will have you living your life:

- apart from God
- out of God's will
- beneath your potential
- void of joy, blessings, and inner peace
- negatively affecting the lives of those around you

Of course, this would cause your journey in life to be a hardship that it was never intended to be.

Jonah was a prophet of the Old Testament whom God had instructed to go to the city of Nineveh and warn the people there about His judgment against them due to their wickedness. Jonah, in his disobedience, went the opposite direction of where God had told him to go and hopped onto a ship that was headed to a city called Tarshish. While on the ship, God caused a violent storm to come about that threatened to destroy the ship. The sailors aboard the ship began praying to their gods and tossing items overboard, hoping to lighten their load. All the while, Jonah was asleep at the bottom of the ship. The men aboard finally figured out that Jonah had fled from the presence of God and was the cause of the turmoil. Jonah suggested that they throw him overboard so that the sea would calm down for them. The men were initially hesitant to follow Jonah's instructions, but eventually, they did as he had suggested and the sea became calm. Jonah's disobedience not only had an impact on the people in Nineveh to whom he was called to preach to, but it also impacted those who were around him.

Living a life of disobedience is a selfish act that keeps us outside of God's perfect will and causes us to live lives that are beneath God's best. Once our lives have become fully aligned with God's Word, we are then able to walk in our purpose here on the earth. Jonah had to go into the belly of a whale before he came to his senses and realized that he couldn't outrun God. If God is calling you to do something, don't hesitate to follow His lead. He has your back and will provide you with the provisions needed to perform whatever it is He requires of you. When you look at yourself apart from God, of course, you are not capable of doing what He is calling you to do, but it is only when you look at Him that you can confidently say, *"I can do all things through Christ which strengtheneth me" (Philippians 4:13 KJV).*

Moses was a man who God called to lead the people of Israel out of Egyptian captivity. He was full of excuses as to why he could not do what God was calling him to do. When he received the instruction from God, he asked, *"Who am I to appear before Pharaoh? Who am I to lead the people of Israel out of Egypt"* *(Exodus 3:11 NLT)? "What if they won't believe me or listen to me? What if they say, 'The Lord never appeared to you" (Exodus 4:1 NLT)?* Moses even went on to say, *"O Lord, I'm not very good with words. I never have been, and I'm not now, even though you have spoken to me. I get tongue-tied, and my words get tangled" (Exodus 4:10 NLT).*

There is no excuse when it comes to doing what God requires of you. Obedience is what God seeks from His children. What makes it so great is that He gives us what we need in order to be obedient, because He knows we can't do it by ourselves. God gave Moses the ability to perform many miraculous signs to convince the Pharaoh of Egypt that he had been sent by

Him *(see Exodus 4:2-9 NLT)*. God also used Moses's brother, Aaron (who was well-spoken), to be his mouthpiece to tell Pharaoh whatever He said to Moses *(see Exodus 4:14-16 NLT)*.

If you read throughout Exodus, you will see how Moses submitted himself to be used by God. Although he didn't initially see his seed of potential, God did. When Moses stopped coming up with excuses and hearkened to the call of God, he was then able to walk fully in his God-given purpose.

Chapter 7
FOUR POTENTIAL KILLERS

Do you know that you have an enemy that doesn't want to see you tap into your God-given potential and live in your purpose here on earth? He schemes his way into your mind and into the hearts of the people around you. This is to keep you from believing that you have what it takes to be all you were created to be and to do all you were created to do. Your enemy is Satan and he is definitely "trying" to fulfill his purpose in the earth of stealing, killing, and destroying your potential, your purpose, and your life *(see John 10:10)*. There are four ways in which the enemy tries to kill your potential and they are:

- doubt
- lack of vision

- laziness
- believing your haters

Doubt

Doubt is a tactic of the enemy that he uses to keep you from believing who you are in God. Doubt causes you to not believe that you have greatness on the inside of you that is awaiting manifestation. If allowed, Satan would have you walking around believing that the promises of the God are for everyone but you. He would make you think that your current situation will never change and that there is no way you can be anything more than the man or woman who never went to college, works at a fast food joint and lives paycheck to paycheck. If you get the strength to believe in your seed of potential, he will try to make you think that it will never grow and that it will eventually die as you get older.

Thanks be to God that He has given us power and authority over the enemy. *"For the weapons of our warfare are not carnal but mighty in God for pulling down strongholds, casting down arguments and every high thing that exalts itself against the knowledge of God, bringing every thought into captivity to the obedience of Christ" (2 Corinthians 10:4-5 NKJV).*

As children of God, we must know that we are at war. There is a major battle going on in the spiritual realm that we must be prepared to fight. *"Put on all of God's armor so that you will be able to stand firm against all strategies of the devil. For we are not fighting against flesh-and-blood enemies, but against evil rulers and authorities of the unseen world, against mighty powers in this dark world, and against evil spirits in the heavenly places"* *(Ephesians 6:11-12 NLT).*

Lack of Vision

Proverbs 29:18 says, "Where there is no vision, the people perish." If you can't see where you are going, you will end up going nowhere. In order to have vision, you have to know the will of God; in order to know the will of God, you have to read and study His Word and have a relationship with Him. The enemy knows that if you get a grip on the Word of God and allow it to govern your life, you will be able to see life much clearer through the eyes of God. That means that you will be able to see your purpose, and even though you may not be walking in the full manifestation of it, you will be able to take steps toward it.

The devil wants you to keep your eyes planted on your weaknesses, but in order to avoid this pitfall, you must keep your eyes on God. You must also begin to seek His will, and as you hear Him speak, begin to write down what He is telling you and walk in it.

Over the years, I have learned the power behind having a vision and writing it down. At the beginning of each year, I make it a habit to write down a list of things that I would like to accomplish throughout the year. At the end of that year, I am able to look back and check off the many things that I wrote down that have come to pass. In book of Habakkuk 2:2-3, the Lord says to the prophet *"Write the vision and make it plain upon tables, that he may run that readeth it. For the vision is yet for an appointed time, but at the end it shall speak, and not lie: though it tarry, wait for it; because it will surely come, it will not tarry."*

Laziness

If for some strange reason, you think that your potential is going to maximize itself with you sitting around browsing social media sites, watching television, and sleeping all day, you are sadly mistaken. You have to put in work if you're going to live a life of purpose. That means that each day, you have to do something that is going to help to grow your potential. If God told you that your purpose is to help the homeless, you should start volunteering your time at a local shelter or start your own community outreach organization to help homeless individuals in your area. *Proverbs 19:15* says that *"Lazy people sleep soundly, but idleness leaves them hungry."* You will always live in lack if you are lazy. The world and everything you have the potential to become will pass you by if you don't get up and start making moves. Make no mistake about it, the moves that you make must be ordained by God to produce good fruit, but just trust Him, take a step and give it your best shot. Learn to give God your little effort, so that He can make much out of it.

Believing Your Haters

There are always going to be people who don't want to see you succeed. They will give you every reason they can think of as to why you can't do this or shouldn't do that. Please know that once you begin to walk in your purpose, your haters will multiply. It is important that you see these individuals for who they truly are. They can be killers of your potential if you allow them to be. Use wisdom and allow them to become your motivators.

Sadly enough, some of your biggest haters may be the people closest to you. Even Jesus experienced haters within His hometown. When people saw the power and ability He possessed, they mocked Him saying, *"He's just the carpenter's son, and we know Mary,*

his mother, and his brothers -James, Joseph,
Simon, and Judas. All his sisters live right
here among us. Where did he learn all these
things? And they were deeply offended and
refused to believe in him" (Matthew 13:55-57).

When your haters see your potential being
maximized, they will always try to bring up your
past. They like to linger in the old in order to
keep you from walking in the newness of what
God is doing in your life. If you believe the
hype of what they are saying, you will begin to
see yourself through their eyes and take your
eyes off of God. Consequentially, your potential
would become stagnant.

Know that the devil is your opponent and he
will do anything and use anyone to keep you
visionless, hopeless, slothful, and believing
your naysayers. Keep fighting the good fight of
faith and put on the full armor of God so that

you can fight off the enemy's attacks. Your purpose is worth fighting for!

Chapter 8
PREGNANT WITH PURPOSE

When a woman first conceives, all that is on the inside of her womb is a small embryo. The sex of the baby cannot be identified during this stage until it begins to grow and develop more. Envision purpose as starting off as a small seed on the inside you. We will call that seed potential. In the beginning, it can be hard to determine exactly what your purpose is, but as you grow in the knowledge of God, you will be able to identify it.

Finding out that you are pregnant can be an exciting thing for most people. The idea of life growing on the inside of you can be an amazing feeling. You get a chance to watch your body change and grow as this gift from

God develops into a full term baby awaiting its delivery and entry into the world. You plan and prepare for your new baby throughout the entire pregnancy, eager to embark upon the journey of parenthood. Even though you have an opportunity to find out the sex of the baby when you are four months into your pregnancy, you still won't know how the delivery is going to go or how the baby will be once it arrives. You will most certainly have concerns about having a miscarriage or delivering your baby prematurely. Being pregnant with purpose can yield the same level of excitement and emotions, especially when you don't know what your purpose is. It can cause you to feel frustrated at times because you know that there is something great in you, but you don't know how to get it out. Just as with a natural pregnancy, being pregnant with purpose requires that it be fully developed before it is ready to be pushed out. Everyone is born with purpose and for a purpose. While your exact purpose may be unknown to you right now, you must come to the realization that the ultimate reason for your purpose is to bring glory to God.

When I reflect on the journey to purpose, I like to think about the story of Joseph and his brothers. Joseph was sold into slavery by his brothers, who were jealous of the dream that God had given him. His brothers attempted to abort his dream by having him sold into slavery to the Ishmaelites, who then took him to Egypt and sold him to Potipher. I'm sure Joseph was terrified as he waited for his purpose to be birthed. He knew that God had designed a particular plan and purpose for his life, but he had no idea how it would manifest. Joseph exercised patience and humility during his journey, but most of all, he exercised obedience to God. He shunned away from things that were not acceptable to God, and through his obedience, God began to give him favor with men.

Joseph's dream was the seed of his purpose. As he grew in the Lord and humbled himself, the seed began to grow bigger. He was later able to identify his purpose after being put in charge of the entire land of Egypt. He had to ensure that his family and others continued to have food and survive during the seven years of famine that had come up on the land. *"But don't be upset, and don't be angry with yourselves for selling me to this place. It was God who sent me here ahead of you to preserve your lives. This famine that has ravaged the land for two years will last five more years, and there will be neither plowing nor harvesting. God has sent me ahead of you to keep you and your families alive and to preserve many survivors. So it was God who sent me here, not you! And he is the one who made me an adviser to Pharaoh—the manager of his entire palace and the governor of all Egypt"* (Genesis 45:5-8 NLT).

Right now, your road to purpose may seem like a big jigsaw puzzle. You can't quite figure out how it's all going to come together for something good, but trust and believe that God will see you through to the end as long as you keep your hand in His just as Joseph did.

The closer you get to birthing purpose, the more uncomfortable you begin to feel in your current situation. You begin to become uneasy and unfulfilled as you go about your day-to-day routine. Of course, that routine is pretty much the path you have chosen for yourself. You begin to realize that there is something greater for you to be doing and that you will not be relieved from your discomfort until you give birth to it.

Morning sickness is commonly experienced during the early months of pregnancy. Many women report symptoms of nausea and vomiting with the inability to keep any food down. Others become queasy by the smell of certain scents. In order to combat these aggravating symptoms, most women tend to avoid all triggers. When you're pregnant with purpose, you will begin to notice that you can't run in the same circles that you used to and do the same things that you once did without being repulsed by it. Completely eluding these things will help you to overcome this obstacle.

While you await the birth of purpose, your seed of potential has to go through a period of incubation. If the incubation period is not long, you will deliver prematurely and not walk fully into what God has designed for you. In the previous chapter, we talked about timing. God's timing is perfect. Anything delivered outside of His timing will not function the way it is supposed to. The correlation to premature babies is the exact same. Preemies don't have fully developed organs, and as a result, they have to have extra time and attention to grow into fully developed, healthy babies. With that being said, your premature delivery will not thwart your purpose, but it will delay its full manifestation.

There are many reasons as to why women suffer miscarriages during pregnancy, but one of the most obvious is due to the mother's lifestyle. A self-destructive lifestyle filled with bad habits, including drug and alcohol abuse, are sure ways to miscarry. Our lifestyles impact whether or not we will be able to carry our purpose through to its full term. If our lives are not lining up with the Word of God, we are not creating a spiritually healthy environment for our potential and purpose to thrive in. Just as an egg and sperm connect to create a fetus, so does the Spirit of God have to connect with our potential to manifest purpose.

Doctors advise pregnant women and those who want to become pregnant to take prenatal vitamins to help provide proper nutrients to the fetus in order to aid in its growth. They suggest diet modifications to those who have not been consuming healthy foods and encourage exercise to keep the body strong as it prepares for the birthing process and thereafter. If you are consuming junk from the world and not feasting on the goodness of God's Word and allowing it shape and prepare you for delivery of your purpose, you will have a difficult journey.

When you know that God has a call on your life and you are running from it like Jonah, you are in the process of aborting your purpose. Even though its seed may appear to be small, your purpose is alive at every stage of its growth. You may be trying to abort it because you don't feel like you're capable of fulfilling the role or you may feel like your external circumstances will never allow you to be in a position to nurture what is on the inside of you. All of these reasons are lies that the enemy will try to have you believe because he knows that what you have on the inside is going to stomp on his head and bring glory to God.

New mothers go through a nesting phase right before giving birth, in which they go on a cleaning and organizing frenzy. This is a natural instinct that they have to ensure that everything is in order for the new life that is coming into the world. Once you face the reality that you're pregnant, you must start to prepare for the birth. You have to start rearranging your environment by getting rid of all the junk and clutter that could get in the way of your purpose. This includes negative relationships, unforgiveness, bitterness, and bad habits.

I think the biggest complaint among pregnant women is the fact that their bodies change. During pregnancy, the body gets bigger and becomes covered with stretch marks. It's not as appealing to the masses as it once was before the pregnancy. People will talk about how the woman's body looks and how she may not be as attractive as she was before she became pregnant. It becomes the woman's desire to get her pre-pregnancy body back at all costs after the delivery. When you are pregnant with purpose, you will change. You are not going to appear the same to those around you. They will notice something different in the way that you talk and the things that you do. Your stretchmarks will come in the form of the struggles and trials that you have to face as your potential grows and shapes into purpose on the inside of you. These stretchmarks are nothing to be ashamed of, as they will serve as reminder of how strong you truly are.

Most pregnant women can't seem to fit in their old clothes anymore because of their growth, and as a result, they have to buy new ones. As you prepare for the birth of your purpose, you will not fit into the same crowds that you were in before. The way you see yourself and your mindset about life will be too big for this old group of people. If you try to force yourself to hang out with the old crowd, it will be as uncomfortable as trying to fit into a pair of size 10 skinny jeans when you truly wear a size 24.

Learn to enjoy this phase of life because its reward is great and worth all of what you have to endure, even though the process may be uncomfortable at times. At this stage, you are glowing. The presence of God is upon you. It's almost time to start pushing!

Chapter 9
LABOR PAINS

When labor pains start to occur, you know that you have entered the last leg of the race. Labor is a very exhaustive process that varies from person to person in regards to intensity of pain and length of time in which one has to endure it. Regardless of whether you're birthing a boy or a girl, a business or a book, labor pains cannot be avoided. It is your body's way of telling you that your baby is soon to be delivered. Some women are able to deliver quickly, while others stay in labor for hours... sometimes days. When it comes to birthing purpose, you may be in labor for years. We must not forget that we operate in God's perfect timing and not our own, so when we deliver our purpose, it will be fully developed and lacking nothing.

The pain of labor is unmatched. It will have you squirming, screaming, crying, and doing anything you possibly can to speed up the process. Some people opt for an epidural for relaxation and pain control. For some, an epidural seems to help, but for others, it doesn't help much. They still experience some break through pain and have a difficult time being at ease. When birthing purpose, you have to learn to relax in God through His Holy Spirit. Now this does not exempt you from experiencing some discomfort, but His Spirit takes the sting of pain away and provides comfort and victory that you would not have experienced if you tried to go at it alone (see 1 Corinthians 1:55-57).

Natural child birth is starting to become a thing of the past. In our world today, everyone wants things to be convenient and easy with the least amount of stress and strain as possible. When it comes to birthing purpose, the best way to deliver is to do it naturally. Although this option may be thought of as the most painful way, in all honesty, it is the best way. It forces you to relinquish control and rest fully upon the power of God to bring to pass what He has placed inside of you.

During the natural birthing process, you will need a midwife by your side to help you get into position and push when it's time to give birth. Due to the immense amount of pain you may be in, you will likely squirm, lose your footing and get out of place, but your midwife will be there to guide you back. Your midwife has to be an individual who is a believer in the faith. Someone who is not a believer will doubt that there is anything to push out and will discourage you from getting into position. As a result, they could easily cause you and your purpose to die. The midwife that you need will be one who will pray for you and encourage you when the labor pain becomes too difficult to bear. He or she will make sure that your purpose is not in breach, and if it is, they will help to re-position you so that it manifests properly. Your midwife will help you get everything prepared for delivery and will teach you how to nurture and fuel your purpose once it has arrived.

It is natural to get tired and want to quit when you are nearing the end of a race and can't see the finish line. The same is true in when it's almost time to push out your purpose. You begin to feel tired and want to quit, but you have your midwife on the sideline cheering you on and telling you that they can see your purpose crowning. Now is not the time to tense up and become afraid, but it is the time to relax, breath, and P.U.S.H (pray until something happens).

Chapter 10
P.U.S.H.

According to Lamaze International, the purpose of Lamaze classes is to "increase women's confidence in their ability to give birth." This class teaches women how to breathe properly and respond to pain. Now that it's time for you to start pushing out this new life of purpose, you have to activate your own spiritual Lamaze, which is prayer. Prayer is the most powerful tool that God has given us to connect to Him. It gives us the power to push through some of the most difficult and most painful times in our lives. 1 Thessalonians 5:17 tells us to *"pray without ceasing"* or in other words P.U.S.H (pray until something happens).

There is tremendous power that is made available to us in prayer. Through prayer, those who are sick are healed, broken marriages are restored, the lost are found, relationships are strengthened, purpose is revealed, peace is given, addiction is overcome, and the list goes on and on. Prayer gives us the power to accomplish things we never thought were possible. The Bible is filled with stories of people who experienced the awesome and miraculous power of prayer. Some of the stories that stick out the most to me include that of Hezekiah, Peter, Hannah, and Jabez.

Hezekiah

Hezekiah was a king of Judah whose ways were pleasing in the sight of the Lord. He placed his trust in the Lord and was careful to follow His commandments. As a result, the Lord was with him and caused him to prosper wherever he went (see 2 Kings 18:3-7). During his reign as king, Hezekiah became deathly ill. The prophet Isaiah prophesied to him that he would not recover from his illness, but would die. Hezekiah prayed to God for healing from his sickness and recounted how he had walked upright before Him. God heard his prayer and healed him, adding fifteen more years to his life (see 2 Kings 20:1-6).

Peter

The Apostle Peter was arrested and locked in prison by King Herod and ordered to be guarded by a total of sixteen soldiers. According to Acts 12:5, while he was in prison, the church fervently and persistently prayed for him. God heard their prayers, and as a result of their prayers, during the night while Peter was asleep, fastened in chains, and being guarded by the soldiers, an angel of the Lord appeared and led him out of prison. At the time, Peter thought that he was seeing a vision, as everything that was happening to him was so miraculous (see Acts 12:6-9).

Hannah

The book of 1 Samuel 1:1-10 speaks of Hannah, the wife of Elkanah, who was barren. She eagerly desired to have a son, so she prayed, *"O Lord of Heaven's Armies, if you will look upon my sorrow and answer my prayer and give me a son, then I will give him back to you. He will be yours for his entire lifetime, and as a sign that he has been dedicated to the Lord, his hair will never be cut" (1 Samuel 1:11 NLT).*

"When Elkanah slept with Hannah, the Lord remembered her plea, and in due time, she gave birth to a son. She named him Samuel, for she said, "I asked the Lord for him" (1 Samuel 1:19-20 NLT).

Jabez

The Bible speaks of a man named Jabez, whose prayer to God has been quoted and prayed many times by many people. In 1 Chronicles 4:10, Jabez, prayed to the God of Israel, *"Oh, that you would bless me and expand my territory! Please be with me in all that I do, and keep me from all trouble and pain!"* And God granted him his request.

While these are just a few of the many biblical examples of answered prayers, there are prayers being answered every day that yield great encouragement to those who hear about them. Recently, I attended a New Years' Eve church service and heard the testimonies of people who had been healed from cancer, HIV, and a host of other things. These testimonies served as a reminder of the awesome, insurmountable power of prayer to an Almighty God.

When I think of Lamaze, I envision pregnant women who are near their delivery date, practicing breathing techniques that will be instrumental in helping facilitate them to be able to push their babies out. Prayer is like breathing; we are supposed to do it without stopping. If you were to stop breathing for approximately three to five minutes, you could suffer irreversible brain damage. If you stop praying, you suffer damage to your relationship with God, as well as to other areas of your life, including your purpose.

As we compare prayer to breathing, there may come a time when you have difficulty breathing on your own and may need oxygen supplementation in the form of a prayer intercessor. Intercessors pray on your behalf when you don't have the strength or know how to pray for yourself. Jesus is the great Intercessor. He stands in the gap between man and God. *"For there is only one God and one Mediator who can reconcile God and humanity —the man Christ Jesus" (1 Timothy 2:5 NLT). "Christ Jesus died for us and was raised to life for us, and he is sitting in the place of honor at God's right hand, pleading for us" (Romans 8:34 NLT).*

Without Jesus, we are not worthy to come before the throne of God. If we attempted to plead our case before God without the blood of Jesus, we would lose.

As believers. we are all called to intercede for one another. I personally know that there have been many times in my life when situations could have turned out negatively for me, but because someone was interceding on my behalf, God turned it around for my good. The book of Ezekiel speaks of a time in which God sought someone to stand in the gap for the people of Israel, but He could find no one, so

He destroyed the land. *"I looked for someone who might rebuild the wall of righteousness that guards the land. I searched for someone to stand in the gap in the wall so I wouldn't have to destroy the land, but I found no one. So now I will pour out my fury on them, consuming them with the fire of my anger. I will heap on their heads the full penalty for all their sins. I, the Sovereign Lord, have spoken!"* (Ezekiel 22:30-31 NLT)

We have to be willing to pray for more than just ourselves and our purpose. We are able to do this by becoming selfless in our prayer lives and placing the needs of others on the altar.

It is essential to know the Word of God for yourself because it is through the Word of God that you know how to pray and what to ask for in prayer. John 15:7 says, *"But if you remain in me and my words remain in you, you may ask for anything you want, and it will be granted!"*

We have to be sure that what we are asking for is lining up with what God says. We must get into agreement with what God says about our lives and remind Him of His promises to us.

Don't stop praying and don't stop pushing until your purpose comes out kicking and screaming. When you first deliver it, it may not look like what you thought it would. You might even think that it doesn't belong to you. Just like a new parent, you will need help from your midwife and others with experience who will be able to give you advice and coach you through the sleepless nights that you will endure in the beginning. You're going to feel tired and weak from pushing out something so great that you may have had to carry for many years. Trust and believe that God will replenish you and give you the strength that you need to carry on. It is in our weakness that God is able to do His greatest work in our lives. You must look to

Jesus during these times in which you may feel tattered and as though you are not capable of fulfilling the purpose that you have been called to.

You must stay in prayer as you birth your purpose. You must ask God to cover you and your purpose, as well as everyone who will be impacted by it. Through prayer, you must ask God to thwart off any schemes that the devil may be trying to perform to cause you to deliver a stillborn purpose. A stillborn purpose is one that has lost connection to its life source...God. While your purpose is still growing on the inside of you, it is receiving life-sustaining nutrients from the Word of God, prayer, and time spent in worship and thanksgiving.

Your enemy knows that your time for delivery of purpose is drawing near and that if your purpose becomes alive in the earth, it will be another weapon used to tear down his kingdom. So, he will do all that he can during this time to disconnect you from God. He will have you doubting what's on the inside of you, getting angry with God because of the process and pain that you're having to go through, and make you want to give up all together. Do not retreat in fear and cower because of the lies that the enemy is feeding you. Instead, utilize your most powerful weapon of prayer, in which you speak to your Father in heaven and ask Him to guide and protect you so that you can fulfill the great and mighty work that He has assigned to you.

Chapter 11
SIX HINDRANCES TO PRAYER

While we have discussed the power and importance of prayer, it is essential that you understand that there are certain behaviors that will prevent your prayers from being answered. No matter how much you P.U.S.H., your prayers will not be heard by God, if you:

- worry
- have unconfessed sin
- pray with wrong motives
- pray outside of God's will
- are ungrateful
- live with unforgiveness

Worry

Worry is a form doubt that shows you don't trust God to do what He said He would do. It's like giving Him a problem and then taking it back because you think that your worrying will help solve the issue. You have to completely surrender your problems to God in prayer and allow Him to work it out in His perfect timing. God doesn't need our help with anything. Learn to let go and let God do what He does best. *Philippians 4:6-7 says, "Don't worry about anything; instead, pray about everything. Tell God what you need, and thank him for all he has done. Then you will experience God's peace, which exceeds anything we can understand. His peace will guard your hearts and minds as you live in Christ Jesus."*

Unconfessed sin

We are all guilty of sin and there are some sins that may even be unintentional. Nonetheless, we must know that sin separates us from God and from Him hearing us. Psalms 66:18-19 says, *"If I had not confessed the sin in my*

*heart, the Lord would not have listened. But
God did listen! He paid attention to my prayer."*

In my personal prayer time, I try to make it a
habit to ask God for forgiveness before I open
my mouth to ask Him for anything else. There
may be things that I may have thought or said
under my breath during my day that were
displeasing to Him. I know I have to frequently
ask for forgiveness while I am driving, as I find
myself saying and thinking things that are not
Christ-like about other drivers. God knows that
we are not perfect. He expects us to
acknowledge our faults and imperfections and
come to Him so that He can cleanse us of our
unrighteousness. This is what is necessary for
the lines of communication to remain open so
that our prayers will be answered.

Wrong Motives

God searches the heart of man and knows
when we are praying with the wrong motives.

Wrong motives are anything that yields selfish gain and does not bring glory to God. It would be selfish and wicked for you to pray for someone to lose their job so that you can take their position or to pray that someone's relationship ends so that you can be with whomever they're with. With each prayer we pray, we need to ask ourselves the following questions:

- Why am I praying for this?
- Will my answered prayers bring glory to God or to myself?

If your answer to these questions center only around you, you have left God out of the mix and you need to ask Him to cleanse your heart and purify your motives. James 4:2-3 says, *"Yet you don't have what you want because you don't ask God for it. And even when you ask, you don't get it because your motives are all wrong—you want only what will give you pleasure."* Be sure to do a heart check before you go to God in prayer.

Praying Outside of God's Will

Don't try to glorify yourself by asking God to give you what "you" want. Make sure that what you are asking for lines up with His will. Reading and studying the bible is a sure way to know what God's good and perfect will is. His Word is His will, therefore, it is important to pray the Word of God to backup whatever it is you are asking Him for. Many times, when I am unsure of what the Word of God says about a personal situation that I may be faced with, I ask God to let His will be done. Praying this way takes my desires out of the equation and only leaves room for what God wants for me. 1 John 5:14-15 says, *"And we are confident that he hears us whenever we ask for anything that pleases him. And since we know he hears us*

when we make our requests, we also know
that he will give us what we ask for."

Ungratefulness

When people show appreciation for the things
you have done for them, it makes you inclined
to want to do more for them. On the other
hand, when you have poured yourself out to
someone and they complain and are
ungrateful, it honestly makes you not want to
deal with them anymore. I'll be the first to admit
that I am definitely grateful that God has
blessed me with a career that provides me with
many opportunities for work. However, on
several occasions, I have found myself
complaining about going to work and
sometimes, wishing I didn't have to go. I have
to stop myself, repent and ask God to forgive
me for complaining and being ungrateful
because there is some man or woman out
there who wishes that he or she had a job to

get up and go to. If we are not grateful over the things that God has blessed us with now, why would He answer our prayers to bless us with more? Like the Apostle Paul, we need to learn to be content no matter what state we find ourselves in. *"For I have learned how to be content with whatever I have. I know how to live on almost nothing or with everything. I have learned the secret of living in every situation, whether it is with a full stomach or empty, with plenty or little" (Philippians 4:11-12 NLT).*

Unforgiveness

I will speak for myself in saying that I fall short daily, and because of this, I know that I need forgiveness daily. I realize that without God being merciful and forgiving me, I would never make it into the Kingdom of God. If I chose not to forgive my brother or sister for something they did to me or someone else, I would be taking advantage of the mercy and grace that God has given me. Because of this, I could not expect Him to forgive me of my trespasses. In the model prayer Matthew 6:12 says, *"And forgive us our sins, as we have forgiven those who sin against us."* You have to make sure that all grudges are dropped and all hard feelings are resolved between you and others before you come to the throne of God in prayer. The disputes that we as individuals have may seem large in our eyes, but they are small and petty in the eyes of God. As messed up as we can be and as crazy as we act at times, we all need Jesus to forgive us. He is so loving and merciful that there is nothing that we can do that He won't forgive (except blasphemy of the Holy Spirit). Don't let unforgiveness block your mouth from reaching God's ears in prayer.

Prayer gives life to your purpose. When your prayer life is non-existent or being impeded by ways that are not pleasing to God, it renders you ineffective and powerless. Choose today to have a two-way relationship with God. Talk to Him and be still before Him so that you can hear His voice and receive instruction as you walk in your purpose.

Chapter 12
HOW TO FUEL YOUR POTENTIAL

The potential that you have may seem small to you right now. The purpose that you are birthing may seem small too, but little is much when it is placed in the hands of the Almighty God. Your purpose is not small when you add God to the mix. He is the fuel to the fire that's on the inside of you. Just as a car cannot run without fuel, you cannot function in your purpose without God. The story of the first disciples comes to mind when I think of how we are when we try to live a life of purpose, devoid of God. James, John, and Simon (Peter) were all fishermen for a living. The book of Luke 5:4-11 recounts how these men had toiled the night before trying to catch fish, but had been unsuccessful. When Jesus came on the scene, He told them to cast their nets into the deep waters to catch some fish. Even though the men had failed earlier at this task, they were obedient to what He instructed them to do and caught so many fish that their nets began to break and their boats almost sank. Immediately, the men realized the awesome power of Jesus and humbled themselves before Him. He then called them to become fishers of men, instead of fish. These men did not hesitate to surrender their lives to Jesus and become obedient to the call and purpose that He had for them.

When God ignites your purpose, there is no limit to what you can do. The job that the disciples had before they allowed Jesus to lead them, was preparing them for their purpose. Their jobs as fishermen had taught them patience, as they had to put the bait out in the water and wait patiently for the fish to take hold of it. Sometimes, they would catch some and sometimes, they would not, but they continued to show up every day regardless of the previous day's outcome. I'm sure God saw their patience and persistence with the fish as potential that could be used for winning souls for the Kingdom of God.

Moses didn't initially realize the potential that God had placed on the inside of him. He came from a background in which he was raised apart from his Hebrew people after being adopted by Pharaoh's daughter (see Exodus 2:1-10). To make matters worse, he had a speech impediment that made him feel self-conscious about speaking in front of others (see Exodus 4:10). The one thing that Moses did have that God used was a love for his people, the Hebrews. This was demonstrated when he killed an Egyptian that he saw beating one of his fellow Hebrews (see Exodus 2:11-

12) and during another time when he tried to break up a fight between two Hebrew men (see Exodus 2:13-14). Moses had a heart for his people that matched that the heart of God and God was able to use the potential that was on the inside of him to lead the people of Israel out of Egypt and into the promise land (see Exodus 3:7-10).

The life of Saul provides another example of what happens when potential is used by God. Saul was a devout Jew who was a firm believer in the Old Testament teachings. He believed that Christianity was a direct conflict with his belief system and as a result, he spent his time zealously persecuting Christians. This included having them arrested and stoning them to death.

One day, Saul was on his way to a town called Damascus, where he planned to detain

Christians and imprison them. On the way there, Saul encountered the divine presence of God and it brought him to the ground. He heard the voice of the Jesus saying, *"Saul! Saul! Why are you persecuting me?" (Acts 9:3 NLT)*. He later got up from the ground, but was unable to see. A believer named Ananias received a message from the Lord, instructing him to go and deliver a message to Saul. *"Go, for Saul is my chosen instrument to take my message to the Gentiles and to kings, as well as to the people of Israel. And I will show him how much he must suffer for my name's sake" (Acts 9:15-16 NLT)*.

Ananias did as the Lord instructed and laid his hands on Saul saying, *"Brother Saul, the Lord Jesus, who appeared to you on the road, has sent me so that you might regain your sight and be filled with the Holy Spirit. Instantly something like scales fell from Saul's eyes, and he regained his sight. Then he got up and was baptized" (Acts 9:17-18 NLT).* From that point on, Saul began preaching about Jesus and his name was later changed to Paul. God used the zeal that Saul had for persecuting Christians and turned it into zeal for building up the Kingdom of God.

God knows the purpose in which He has created all of us and He uses the most unseemly things to bring glory to His Kingdom. He takes the things that we see as weaknesses and turns them into our strengths. *"My grace is all you need. My power works best in weakness." So now I am glad to boast about my weaknesses so that the power of Christ can work through me. That's why I take pleasure in my weaknesses, and in the insults, hardships, persecutions, and troubles that I suffer for Christ. For when I am weak, then I am strong" (2 Corinthians 12:9-10 NLT).*

Our potential is based upon the way we perceive ourselves and it cannot be fueled until we see ourselves as God sees us. All of the biblical greats that we read about had limitations and had a difficult time tapping into their potential and seeing themselves as God saw them. Gideon, who was one of the judges of Israel, didn't initially see himself as a mighty man of valor who had the backing of the Lord. He didn't understand why the Israelites were being defeated by the Midianites if God was truly with them. God told him something very profound and it is important for us to grasp it as well. He told him to, *"Go with the strength you have, and rescue Israel from the Midianites. I am sending you!" (Judges 6:14 NLT)*
We have very little strength, but when the Almighty is with us, there isn't anything that we can't do. In other words, your potential may be small, but when it is backed by God, you become mighty through Him. Even with God

telling Gideon that He had his back, Gideon still looked at himself and questioned his ability based on his weaknesses. God assured him once more that he would make what appeared impossible to him possible. *"But Lord,"* Gideon *replied, "how can I rescue Israel? My clan is the weakest in the whole tribe of Manasseh, and I am the least in my entire family!" The Lord said to him, "I will be with you. And you will destroy the Midianites as if you were fighting against one man" (Judges 6:15-16 NLT).*

Humility in acknowledging God as your source helps you to access potential and operate in purpose. If Gideon had thought that he could take on the Midianites by himself, he would've failed and many lives would have been negatively impacted by it. The call and pursuit of purpose have high stakes involved. Those stakes involve the lives of others and not fulfilling God's ultimate plan for your life in the earth. Your purpose adds value to other people's lives. We have to partner with God in the pursuit of purpose. If you try to pursue it on your own, you will most definitely miscarry. *Christ is the solid rock on which you must stand; all other ground is sinking sand.*

Chapter 13
CONNECTED FOR PURPOSE

Be encouraged on this journey. Know that you are not alone. God is with you and will send the help that you need to walk into your purpose and live your purpose with tenacity and fervor. With God's grace, do everything with great intention and make purposeful decisions and connections that will be edifying to the Kingdom of God. It is important to realize that not every relationship that you have is directly connected to your purpose. Some people are in your life for a season, while others are there for a lifetime. Those who are present for a season can play a part in planting a seed that you need in order to grow in a particular area of your life. At the same time, there are some seasonal relationships that can be counterproductive to growth. Any relationship that is keeping you from going in the direction in which God has intended for you is one that you have to get out of. Be sure not to sleep on the enemy. You have to realize that he is very strategic in doing whatever it takes to keep you from your purpose and destiny. He will start attacking you more and will place people in your life that initially appear to have good intentions, but when the time comes, they will tear you apart if you don't use discernment and if you allow them to stick around too long.

You also have to be careful not to isolate yourself from relationships altogether in fear of being hurt or misused. It is God's intent that we be connected in relationships. We were created for connection. First and foremost, God created us to be connected to Him. We have this connection through the blood that was shed by Jesus Christ on the cross. Psalms 1:1-

3 highlights the importance of having proper connections. The scripture says, *"Blessed is the man that walketh not in the counsel of the ungodly, nor standeth in the way of sinners, nor sitteth in the seat of the scornful. But his delight is in the law of the LORD; and in his law doth he meditate day and night. And he shall be like a tree planted by the rivers of water, that bringeth forth his fruit in his season; his leaf also shall not wither; and whatsoever he doeth shall prosper."* When you turn from ungodly influences and seek a relationship with God through His Word, He will make sure that you remain secure in Him. He will ensure that you never thirst and that you live a fruitful life as you remain connected to Him.

It is important to know that you cannot bring forth anything if you are not connected to a life source. Water is synonymous with the Word of God. It is the source of life and the foundation of all creation. It is the one thing in the natural that you can't live without, just as spiritually, you cannot live without the Bread of Life, which is the Word of God. In the natural, you can live without food for at least forty days, but you can only live without water for three days. In the spiritual sense, you are a dead man walking if you are existing in the world without the Living Water from the Word of God. Relationship with the Father is the only way your purpose is going to be fulfilled.

The cross represents the vertical relationship that mankind needs to have with our Savior Jesus Christ, but it also represents the horizontal relationships that we need to have with one another. Ecclesiastes teaches us that it is not wise to be without relationships. When it speaks of a three cord strand not being easily broken, it means that two individuals who have a relationship in which God is in the midst cannot be torn apart.

"Two people are better off than one, for they can help each other succeed. If one person falls, the other can reach out and help. But someone who falls alone is in real trouble. Likewise, two people lying close together can keep each other warm. But how can one be warm alone? A person standing alone can be attacked and defeated, but two can stand back-to-back and conquer. Three are even better, for a triple-braided cord is not easily broken" (Ecclesiastes 4:9-12 NLT).

You need God appointed relationships to help you reach your potential and purpose. When God puts something in you, it takes others to help you get it out. The same goes when you are having a baby. You need someone to help encourage you to push it out. You need the doctor to check up on you to ensure that the baby is growing the way it is supposed to. You need someone to help you prepare the environment for the baby's arrival. I know there are cases when some people deliver babies on their own and do all of the things that I mentioned without help from others, but this is not the way God intended for it to be. You can try to do things in an isolated state without having purposeful relationships, but it honestly is going to lead to a lot of unnecessary heartache and pain. I remember hearing a pastor say that if you have a vision that you can accomplish on your own, it's not truly a vision. A vision or purpose requires the help of others. If it's something you can do on your own, you may become pompous and give credit to yourself, instead of giving glory to God.

In Chapter 25 of the book of Exodus, God gave Moses instructions to build the Tabernacle. He provided him with a plan for its design, told him the exact type of material that needed to be used to build it, and He gave him the building's dimensions. Now, Moses was not a carpenter or a designer, and he didn't have the resources to build the Tabernacle, but God placed the right people in his path to do the work, and the resources were supplied by the people of Israel whose hearts were moved to give (see Exodus 25:2).

After giving Moses extensive and intricate details regarding the design, dimensions, and resources needed to build the Tabernacle, its sacred items, and priestly garments, God specifically told Moses who He had chosen to be the craftsmen for this great task.

Then the Lord said to Moses, "Look, I have specifically chosen Bezalel son of Uri, grandson of Hur, of the tribe of Judah. I have filled him with the Spirit of God, giving him great wisdom, ability, and expertise in all kinds of crafts. He is a master craftsman, expert in working with gold, silver, and bronze. He is skilled in engraving and mounting gemstones and in carving wood. He is a master at every craft! "And I have personally appointed Oholiab son of Ahisamach, of the tribe of Dan, to be his assistant. Moreover, I have given special skill to all the gifted craftsmen so they can make all the things I have commanded you to make: the Tabernacle; the Ark of the Covenant; the Ark's cover—the place of atonement; all the furnishings of the Tabernacle; the table and its utensils; the pure gold lampstand with all its accessories; the incense altar; the altar of burnt offering with all its utensils; the washbasin with its stand; the beautifully stitched garments—the sacred garments for Aaron the priest, and the garments for his sons to wear as they minister as priests; the anointing oil; the fragrant incense for the Holy Place. The craftsmen must make everything as I have commanded you" (Exodus 31:1-11).

This is what I consider to be a purposeful connection. If Moses had attempted to build the temple alone, it would have been a complete and utter mess because it was not a part of the plan in which God called him to do. God gave him the vision and others were assigned to provide the provision and put in the work to make it come to pass. Ask God to help you build your life and to finish what He has given you to build by placing the right connections in your path.

Chapter 14
DON'T GIVE UP

Success is failure turned inside out -
The silver tint of the clouds of doubt,
And you never can tell how close you are -
It may be near when it seems afar;
So stick to the fight when you're hardest hit -
It's when things seem worst that you mustn't
quit.
- by Author Unknown

The fulfillment of your purpose is not going to
happen without there being some bumps and
hiccups along the way. Rest assured that God
will use every bump and every hiccup for your
good and His glory. Nothing that you have
gone through, whether good or bad, will be
wasted. "*And we know that God causes*

everything to work together for the good of those who love God and are called according to his purpose for them" (Romans 8:28 NLT). No matter how difficult the journey to purpose becomes, always know that *"The Lord will work out the plans for your life" (Psalms 138:8).* As we discussed in Chapter 8, Joseph's journey to fulfilling his purpose was full of mountaintop and valley experiences. Ultimately, it all worked out to bless him and to help him be a blessing to the glory of God. The journey to fulfilled purpose can be daunting. There will be times when you just don't understand what God is going to do and how He's going to do it. It is during these times of frustration that we must wait patiently on the Lord. *Isaiah 30:18* says, *"For the Lord is a faithful God. Blessed are those who wait for his help."* Help is on the way. Don't give up and succumb to living a life that God never intended for you live.

God has greatness on the inside of you that is eager to burst forth into the world. It is important that we wait for God with great anticipation. This means that we trust Him throughout the entire process, knowing that even though we can't see what He is doing, we believe that He is working behind the scenes for our good.

When I think of waiting with anticipation, it reminds me of how I used to feel as a kid the night before Christmas. My parents would wait the night before Christmas to wrap up the bulk of our gifts. Even though the gifts under the tree were scarce the weeks prior to Christmas, I knew without a doubt that when I woke up Christmas morning, there would be more gifts under the tree. My confidence in this came from what my parents had done in the past, so I could rest easy and with great anticipation, knowing that there would be plenty of gifts to open on Christmas morning. As believers seeking the purpose of God, we have to look at God's track record with everything else He has done in our lives. I am able to look back on the fact that when money has been low, God has never left me unable to pay a bill or eat. I can reflect back on how when my heart was broken from divorce and I never thought that I could heal and love again, God healed my heart and made me whole in His love. When I couldn't understand my purpose and His awesome plan for my life, He began to speak to my heart, and from that, this book was birthed. I know that God loves me and He loves you too. He didn't take His time making such beautiful creations out of His likeness to be useless in the earth.

Progress

Be deliberate about making progress. God is a God of progression, not of stagnation. Progress opens you to fresh opportunities and new challenges. If a baby gave up trying to walk after his or her first fall, that baby would never make progress and develop the way in which God intended for him or her to. I'm sure babies get hurt when they fall, but they keep getting back up and trying over and over again until they are able to do what God intended for them to do: walk, move, and progress. Even as you wait on God, you can still be actively waiting and making progress by worshipping Him, spending time in His presence, and meditating on His word. The bible says that your strength is renewed while you wait. *"But they that wait upon the LORD shall renew their strength; they shall mount up with wings as eagles; they shall run, and not be weary; and they shall walk, and not faint"* (Isaiah 40:31 KJV).

God's Will

As you follow God's will for your life, there is no possible way you can or will fail. For me, knowing that I am doing what is in His will for my life keeps me from wanting to give up. Knowing that your Heavenly Father has your back makes you want to keep going and keep pushing because you know that when it gets too tough, He is right there to pick you up and carry you the rest of the way on the journey. When you are going about things outside of God's will, you will not have the stamina that is necessary to keep going. You will give up. I am at the point in my life now where I don't want anything that God doesn't want for me. I don't care how spectacular it may be or how awesome I think it is. If it doesn't have my Father's stamp of approval on it, I don't want any part of it. This is the mentality that we all must have to fulfill our purpose. Either you are going to follow God's will or your own. The two are oftentimes in direct conflict with one another. There is only one way that leads to the Kingdom of God and that is God's way.

Comfort Vs. Challenge

Don't chose comfort over challenge.

Sometimes, we have to be made to feel uncomfortable in order for us to start moving in the direction that God has destined for us to go in. Be sure not to use your discomfort in situations as a reason to give up. Many times, I have thought about staying in certain positions, because they were easy and felt comfortable. I would feel a nudge on the inside of me trying to get me to move into a new area, but I would be too afraid of stepping out of the proverbial comfort zone. Comfort does not produce growth, but atrophy. Think of comfort as being sedentary and discomfort as being the resistance needed to fuel the growth of your potential. Don't be afraid and don't give up when things become different from your norm. One day, you will be able to look back and see how strong you've become when what you thought was a challenge before suddenly becomes easy.

Preparation

Benjamin Franklin once said, *"When you fail to plan, you plan to fail."* This is a quote that I truly believe and think is essential to implement along the journey to purpose. Planning or preparation gives you a road map to guide you in whatever you do and wherever you go. For example, when it comes to dieting and eating healthy, many people do meal prep at the start of each week. This helps to ensure that they are not tempted to get off track and eat some of the savory unhealthy foods that they may come across on their journeys to better health. Without meal preparation, they are likely to gorge out on chips and cookies when they want a snack, instead of reaching for the apple and almonds that they have set aside for their daily indulgence. As you walk in your purpose

or even as you seek your purpose, you must
prepare for each day ahead by spending time
at the feet of God. This is the only tried and
proven way to ensure that you have what you
need to stay on track and thwart off the
confusion, discouragement, and all the
negative thoughts that the enemy will try to
throw your way. Just as people bask in the sun
to soak up the nutrients from Vitamin D, you
must bask in the presence of God. Get before
Him, soak up His Spirit and allow it to come in
and transform your life. It will give you the fuel
and the know-how that you need to accomplish
whatever the day calls for. I am a witness that if
this is not done, the spirit of defeat will quickly
try to come in and deter you from what God
has for you.

There is someone in the world right now who is
waiting for you to walk in your purpose. Their
well-being depends on you being obedient to

the call that God has on your life. Someone's sick body is waiting for you to walk in your calling as a doctor. Some innocent person on death row is waiting for you to respond to the call of an of being an attorney or a judge to hear their case and fight on their behalf. Some child with a learning disability is waiting for the compassion and patience of the teacher that you have been called to be. You are going to hurt and it is not going to be easy, but don't stop believing, don't stop fighting, don't stop praying, and most of all, don't give up. God has something so awesome in store for your life that it will cause a paradigm shift in your thinking. *"No eye has seen, no ear has heard, and no mind has imagined what God has prepared for those who love him" (1 Corinthians 2:9 NLT).*

You have to tame your attitude during this process. The way you respond to the ups and downs that will come on the road to purpose will determine if you reach your highest potential. Difficulties are on their way if you haven't already experienced them and good days are on their way too if you haven't experienced them either. Life produces a cycle of ups and downs, but be encouraged that you will never stay down and you won't always stay up. It is during the down times that your strength and your character are built to prepare you for the success that happens during the good days and helps you to keep fighting when you're down.

Be intentional about facing adversity head on. Your muscle to fight the good fight of faith is being developed during these times. Remember that resistance builds strength. You can't think that you are going to have big strong muscles if you never hit the weights. I have tried lifting weights before and it was when I hit those last few reps that I wanted to just drop the weights and quit. Nevertheless, it is in those last few reps when it hurts the most that you get stronger and get the best results.

Don't give up on your purpose by looking at where you are now or where you've been. Keep your eyes and your hope on the things that are to come. Without hope for the future, you will not have the tenacity and fortitude to persist through the trials that life brings. The past is the past and has only served as a stepping stone to bring you to where you are today. Don't allow it to be something that you lean on or a broken crutch that you use, because it will only cause you to stumble and fall.

Chapter 15
YOUR PURPOSE MATTERS FOR ETERNITY

What you are experiencing in your life right now is not all there is to the story of your life. You were created and destined for greatness. As we have discussed throughout the text of this book, you were created for a purpose on this earth that is ultimately designed to bring glory to God. It is very important that you know that your purpose has eternal implications. What this means is that everything that you are doing towards your purpose here on earth is preparing you and others for your eternal destination. If you don't know it by now, let me share with you that once you die and leave this earth, you will either spend eternity in Heaven or Hell. Both places are real and how you live your life will determine which place you go.

As believers, we have all been called to go and be world changers by spreading the Gospel of Jesus Christ. You may ask yourself, "how can I spread the Gospel if I haven't been called to be a preacher or a teacher of the Word?" You can spread the Good News by the way in which you live your life before others. Your actions speak greater volumes than what you say. We are called to be hearers and doers of the Word (see James 1:22).

God's ultimate judgment of us is going to be based on our obedience to His Word and what He has called us to do in this life. If you are seeking out your own will and doing things that God never intended for you to do, don't think that this is pleasing to God. You may even think that what you are doing is pleasing to Him

because you are doing it in His name. For example, if God called you to be a Deacon of the church, but you are functioning as the Pastor of the church, you can't expect God to be pleased because it is outside of the call and purpose that He has predestined for your life. 1 Samuel 15:22 says, *"Obedience is better than sacrifice."* This scripture is taken from a particular account in which God specifically gave Saul instructions to *"Go and completely destroy the entire Amalekite nation- men, women, children, babies, cattle, sheep, goats, camels, and donkeys" (1Samuel 15:3 NLT).* The scripture goes on to say, *"Then Saul slaughtered the Amalekites from Havilah all the way to Shur, east of Egypt. He captured Agag, the Amalekite king, but completely destroyed everyone else. Saul and his men spared Agag's life and kept the best of the sheep and goats, the cattle, the fat calves, and the lambs —everything, in fact, that appealed to them.*

They destroyed only what was worthless or of poor quality" (1 Samuel 15:7-9 NLT).

If you read further in Chapter 15 of 1 Samuel, you will see that Saul intended to take the animals and plunder that he gathered from the Amalekites and bring them to God as a sacrifice. If God did not instruct you to do something, the sacrifice that you offer up to Him will be a stench to His nose and will not be accepted. Rebellion towards God's instruction is the equivalent of witchcraft and stubbornness is as bad as the worship of idols (see 1 Samuel 15:23).

God doesn't want sacrifices of our works. He wants us to give Him a sacrifice of praise (see Hebrews 13:15) and the giving of our body as a living sacrifice (see Romans 12:1). Above all, He wants our obedience. The one and only sacrifice that was needed was paid in full by the blood of Jesus Christ. He put in the work by

carrying our cross and He shed His precious blood in His crucifixion.

Don't live your life so unintentionally that you come to the end of it and God says, *"I never knew you: depart from me, ye that work iniquity" (Matthew 7:23 KJV).* Being in true relationship with God will keep you from going after things that are not for you. Relationship with the Father keeps your ears open and attentive to His voice and promptings.

Be sure that the foundation in which you build your life on is one that can withstand the fire that will come on the day of judgment. Using materials of gold, silver, and jewels to build is the equivalent of building on the foundation of Christ and being obedient to His purpose for your life. Materials such as wood, hay, or straw that are used for constructing your foundation is the same as following your fleshly desires, instead of God's perfect plan for your life (see 1 Corinthians 3:12-15). Motives that are not inclined toward the will and purposes of God will not withstand the testing that is sure to come.

Give me Father, a purpose deep,
 In joy or sorrow Thy word to keep;
Faithful and true what e'er the strife,
Pleasing Thee in my daily life;
Only one life, 'twill soon be past,
Only what's done for Christ will last.
-C.T. Studd

God is the Alpha and the Omega. Your purpose for life begins and ends in Him. It should be the desire of every believer to hear God say, *"Well done, good and faithful servant; thou hast been faithful over a few things, I will make thee ruler over many things: enter thou into the joy of thy lord" (Matthew 25:23 KJV).* God expects to gain interest on the potential that He has placed on the inside of each and every one of us. He wants to see that the little that He has given us was turned into much by placing our complete trust in His perfect plan for our lives.